KEEP IT
SASSY,
AUSTIN!

73

keep it
SASSY!!
AUSTIN!

HOT TEEN SLUT

BY CRISTIN O'KEEFE APTOWICZ

A Write Bloody Book
Long Beach, CA USA

Hot Teen Slut
a collection of poetry

൫

by Cristin O'Keefe Aptowicz

Write Bloody Publishing
America's Independent Press

Long Beach, CA

writebloody.com

Aptowicz, Cristin O'Keefe.
1st edition.
ISBN: 978-1-935904-68-7

Interior Layout by Lea C. Deschenes
Cover Designed by Joshua Grieve
Proofread by Sarah Kay
Edited by Derrick Brown and Sarah Kay
Author Photo by Alex Brook Lynn
Type set in Helvetica by Linotype and Bergamo (www.theleagueofmoveabletype.com)

Special thanks to Lightning Bolt Donor, Weston Renoud

Printed in Tennessee, USA

Write Bloody Publishing
Long Beach, CA
Support Independent Presses
writebloody.com

To contact the author, send an email to writebloody@gmail.com

HOT TEEN SLUT

THE LISTING

GUIDE SERVICE MANAGER

An exciting job at the world's
sixth largest web portal.
Must be a good writer and editor,
be self-motivated and work well
with a variety of independent
freelancers.

Open mind and fun attitude
a plus.

Health insurance and 401K.

Salary commiserates with
experience.

MY MOST MEMORABLE INTERVIEW

There are two of them, two men,
and they are both laughing at my jokes.
Everything is going great.

The office is clean, bustling
with young people. My heart
glitters in my nervous chest:
I could work here.

Then the older one clears his throat,
says, *Now about the job. I'm not sure*
if we have been 100% clear
about what it will entail. You will be
working in our "adult interest section."
Do you know what that means?

This is only my fourth interview
in the five months I've been looking.
I have worn the same outfit
to all my interviews. It is black
and it smells like spilled coffee
and failure.

I'd give anything to know
the right answer to his question.
I'd give anything to have this job.
Instead, I knit my fingers together
and wait for him to explain.

"Adult Interest" means erotica.
We have erotic sites that aren't
really linked to our main homepage,
but we do manage them. They are
our sites. Do you understand so far?

I nod.

Now we use the word "erotica"
because it's nice. But make no mistake:
This is porn.

Now is this something
you are comfortable with?

For the last four months,
I have eaten nothing but frozen pierogies
and day-old pastries scored for free
from my friend Patrick's café.

My savings have been consumed
by NYC rent and resumé paper.

At this point I would be comfortable
with *anything*. So I turn to these men,
these two men who are interviewing me
for a real honest-to-goodness job,
and I say, *Bring on the blow jobs!*

Thank God: they laugh.

The little guy turns to the big guy
and goes, *Well, let's leave her alone*
with the laptop and see how she feels.

Alone in the conference room,
I sip free coffee, soak
in the air conditioning.

I want it.
I want this job.
Bad.

PORN

has nothing to do with love,
in regards to me at least,
except that I love boys
and boys love porn.

SOCKS

A friend of mine told me
that she always wears socks
whenever she has sex,
so that when she finally
does fall in love,
the sex with that guy
will be special.

This is modern life,
and this is why
I am a virgin.

I'D LIKE TO THANK THE ACADEMY

I got the call.
I got the job.
Starting Monday,
I'm working in porn.

I'd like to thank
Robert Honor
at NYU Job Services
for the months of support
and job listings.

I'd like to thank my teachers
at the Tisch Dramatic Writing Program
for the degree in Fine Arts
which said to my new employer:
I can handle porn.

But most of all,
I'd like to thank America,
because its men love porn,
its people love the internet,
and its laws prevent employers
from asking questions
during job interviews
such as:

Hey, seeing as this is a job in porn,
we have to ask: have you ever
actually had sex before?

This year is beginning to look up.

THE FIRST DAY

feels like a lot of other first days.

I tend to size up lobbies. I debate
striking up a friendship with the security guard.
Like a kindergartener, I hope I make friends.

I wear the same outfit I wore
for both interviews. The outfit says,
I am capable of working in an office.
The fact that I've worn it three times
in a row says, *please let me dress down,*
or else you may see a lot of this outfit.

Jordan will be helping me learn the ropes.
Jordan wears a company-issued bowling shirt
and a name tag that says "Hoffmonster."

Jordan's office contains a large sombrero,
a talking *Simpsons* clock, dozens of CDs,
and a sad sack office mate named Will.

On my tour of the office, I am introduced
to people whose names I immediately forget.
I am also shown the break room, which features
a limitless supply of chips, cookies and sodas.

Jordan says that I'll get my computer tomorrow,
but do I have any questions now? No. Okay then.

I sit in air-conditioning, absolutely shining:
my first paycheck in months.

I celebrate by drinking twelve cans of YooHoo
in just under eight hours: a new office record.

AN EDUCATION

The first thing you have to acknowledge is
the fact that you will be looking at porn all day,
every day. People will walk past your desk and
there will be porn on your computer screen.

My boss Jamie looks me in the eyes:

It's important to remember: there should be porn
on your screen. So don't be embarrassed at all.
You need to get over that quick. This is your job.

He takes it easy on me on my first day,
setting me up in a private conference room.
I familiarize myself with the sites, the writers,
how to read the stats page to see what's really
generating all those clicks.

Any terms I don't understand, I look up on Google.
If there are any broken images or broken links,
I am to report them to Jamie.

And of course, the first link I click doesn't work:
Double Penetration.

Jamie only left the room forty-five seconds ago.

I decide not to bother him right away,
but instead make a list I'll send him hourly.
Following that decision, I become paranoid
that my list is becoming telling.

My new strategy becomes:
search the sites picking the opposite
of what my last site was: gay orgy
to lesbian solo masturbation; straight sex
to celebrity screen shots.

Several hours later, I take lunch.
In the breakroom, I can't even look
at a YooHoo.

Jordan walks in, asks how my first day
is going. He eats an enormous sandwich
and I can't help but stare.

Everything is beginning to look
a little strange to me now.

JAMIE

has a ton of kids. Only some are boys,
but they all have haircuts like boys
and they all play sports.

Some of this job involves
checking sites on the weekends
and so he is happy to be passing
the porn sites over to me,
the new editor.

His wife is happy too.

JORDAN

lives in my neighborhood,
went to the same school as me,
and likes to tell you about the food
he is eating. Today he is eating pickles.

Apparently, it's pickle season.
He hand-picked these pickles
from a barrel on Delancey Street
and he says I have to taste them.

He shoves the briny plastic bag
in my direction. I demure, pointing
out that I see quite enough of this action
on my laptop, and it never ends well
for the ladies.

It's an easy joke and a weak joke,
but it's my first one to Jordan,
and he generously applauds.

For the rest of the afternoon,
he pretends to be embarrassed
when I catch him kissing his pickles,
stroking them gently,
calling them by name.

WILL

is in charge of the music sites
and is never without his headphones.
He shares an office with Jordan,
who throws balled-up paper at him
when Jordan wants Will to listen.

Will never wants to listen,
but nonetheless patiently waits
for Jordan to finish his story.

Will has an enormous jaw,
sad eyes, and a friendly flat head.
He reminds me of Frankenberry,
the jolly cereal-based Frankenstein.
This is something I don't say out loud.

At our weekly meetings, Will begins
all of his statements with a sigh.
He looks lost without his headphones.

When I give updates on my sites,
he taps his pen arrhythmically
and never looks me in the eyes.

THE GUY IN CHARGE OF SPORTS

doesn't blink often, but when he does
it's powerful, like he's using every muscle
in his face. BLINK.

He jiggles his legs even when standing,
and when I first met him it took about 35 seconds
before he told me that he had applied for my job.

Behind him I see Jordan and Jamie looking over,
waiting for the right moment to jump in.

Sports Guy doesn't want to be pushy,
and I don't have to answer, but…
How well do I really know porn.
I mean, really? It's cool to answer honestly.

I smile, say, *Hey, I don't know why they hired me.*
Maybe they were just looking for a female voice.
A funny voice.

Funny, he repeats. *Did they tell you that?*

Because Sports Guy? He can be funny.

Jordan walks over and claps a hand
on Sports Guy's shoulder.

Ha ha, leave the poor girl alone.
This guy! Every cute girl in the building!
Ha ha ha!

When Sports Guy wanders away
Jamie slides over and says, *So…*
Did he tell you he wanted your job?

I nod.

Jamie lets out a sigh and looks over
at Sports Guys blinking solidly in his cubicle.

Yeah, well, don't feel bad that you got the job.
He was a good candidate.

But sometimes you can like something so much
you probably shouldn't have a job in it,

you know what I mean?

REAL LIVE PROMO I

Just Do It! </a>
Sex Industry Guides Gary and Kris Booth
give you the lowdown on the real Australian Bush Country!</font></TD>

In the Gym, In the Park, On the Roof...</a>
Adult Swinging Guide Carolee G. shows you
that there isn't a place where groups of people won't fuck!.</font></TD>

Game, Set, Snatch!</a>
Straight Men's Erotica Guide Don Waterman
shows you a bunch of hot links,
including an obscene(ly addictive) tic-tac-toe </font></TD>

DOT COM COOL

Our new office is huge.
We have taken over three stories
in the building, and the outdoor patio,
with its view of Times Square,
is set-up for wireless. Those who
like to smoke while working now
can also work on their tans. Ha-ha.

The reason it took me half a year
to find a job was because the internet boom
is supposed to be dying. But don't tell that to us.

We are resilient, and our twin founders
stand before us all in the new building
reminding us to keep the spirit alive.

That as long as they are around,
we will always have foosball tables,
we will always have free laptops,
we will always be the cutting edge kids,
who will be taking the world by storm,
with pop tarts and free sodas for all.

Amen.

TITTY-FUCK

I didn't even know this
existed until I was 18.

Whoever first thought
this up was a man.

Whoever was the first
woman to consent was
an idiot.

THREE THUMBS UP

That's how the first guy
I ever kissed rated our first kiss.
When I pointed out that
he only had 2 thumbs, he said,
I count my big toes as thumbs!

My God, I thought,
What have I done?

THINGS YOU CAN'T SAY
WHEN YOU WRITE FOR PORN
OR YOUR CO-WORKERS
WILL LAUGH AT YOU

Man, I've been working too long.
My fingers are killing me.

Is it getting hot in this office, or what?

Oh man… is anybody else's keyboard sticky?

So when you say there is a problem with one
of my drives, do you mean the hard one?

What kind of pizza is that? Sausage?
I loooove sausage!

Why is my desk wet?

NEW MILLENNIAL BADASS

Let me tell you something.
When you wake up in the morning,
take a shower, get dressed, go to work,
and the first thing you do is turn on
your computer and look at photos
of two hot, hard guys doing each other
in the mouth and bum, you are either
on the road to getting fired

or you are me.

Let me tell you something.
When that cute guy from tech comes down
to audit your computer for "illegal hardware"
and finds three fisting videos, a *Beginner's
Guide to BDSM*, and the complete trailer
for the film *Ejacula*, and all he can say is:
Well, everything looks to be in order…

then honey, you can be safe
in the assumption that you are
the resident badass.

That's right,
I'm my internet company's
dirty little secret.

I'm the porn girl.

Only one on the floor. Only one in the building.
Only one getting paid cash money
to write copy like:

Panting for Panties:
Let us get you to the brink
with photos of ladies wearing
nothing but wet cotton!

I am getting people to the brink all day long,
and I don't even have to be in the same country as them.

I'm the New Millennial Badass!

Call me up at two in the afternoon,
and I'll tell you the URL where you can watch
Paris Hilton fuck for free.

Break up with your boyfriend,
and I will have him inserted
into an all 'leather daddy' gay erotica story,
where his name will be
the online gloryhole flashpoint
for so many cock-tugging burly bear men
that when he finally goes home
to the girl he broke up with you to be with,
he'll cum HTML all over her Banana Republic
beige tweed skirt.

Oh *yes.*

I'm *that* girl.

I'm the trouble maker.
Piss me off, and guess whose head
will be photoshopped into a threesome
with Dick Cheney and George W. Bush?

I'm so hardcore, that compared to me,
Ron Jeremy is only double X.

I'm so hardcore, that my boss once yelled at me
for looking at CNN.com.

I'm so hardcore, that my computer dictionary
now accepts the words wetty, mangina,
and buttgasm: a word I created *myself*.

And I'm so hardcore, that I write poetry
during my lunch break.

And I'm so hardcore, that I am writing this poem
during my lunch break.

And I'm so hardcore, that I wish my lunch break
lasted all day, because I'd much rather be known
as the poet girl than the porn girl.

But I'm so hardcore, that I live in a country
that only spends 4 cents per citizen on the arts.

And I'm so hardcore, that when I tried to live
on my art alone, I had to budget myself
five pierogies a day just to pay rent.

And I'm so hardcore, that I took the first damn job
that came along and I lucked out with a rock 'n' roll job
where I watch naked people do naked things to each other
all day long and get paid for it.

But I am so hardcore, that I don't even care.

Because no matter how cool working for porn
seems at cocktail parties or at poetry readings,

the truth of the matter is I am being paid
not to write my own stuff for eight hours a day,
forty hours a week. And if that ain't the definition
of "anti-badass," I don't know what is.

But don't worry about me, honey,
because I've got a plan.

And not only that,
I've got a savings account
with a bitching interest rate.

And as soon as I suck off the porn industry
for as much money as I can, until my wallet drips
$100 bills down the insides of my thighs,
then I am kicking porn to the curb
and becoming the real New Millennial Badass.

Writing poetry all day, everyday.
Poetry so hardcore, that when it finally breaks
through that hot white wall of Academia,
all my readers are going to cum in unison
and only in iambic pentameter.

WORK SONG

When I leaned back to yawn
and the headphones I was given
on my first day on the job
popped out of my laptop,

my computer enjoyed
a loud and extended orgasm.

As I struggled to replace the cord,
heads rose out of the surrounding cubicles
like moans out of a heaving chest.

When the headphones were finally
plugged in, the ensuing silence seemed
suddenly louder than sex.

On the screen, the tanned & oily man
in the video stopped pumping for a few seconds
and actually gave me a wink.

PAYDAY

Direct deposit means
this check you are giving me
is all for show.

I kiss it nonetheless.

I.T. GUYS

I am, by far, the favorite editor
of the I.T. guys.

I am on Floor 7,
while all the tech guys work
on Floor 11.

We non-tech-people
are supposed to march up the four flights
to hand our computers over to them,
chirping worriedly about the last moments,
the important files, the impending deadlines.

The I.T. guys, in turn, are supposed
to gaze boredly at us and to not take notes.
They will roughly grab the laptop, turn,
and place it next to a whole pile of laptops.

But when you work in porn,
and you are a girl, and you are funny,
the I.T. guys will find the time
to come down to your floor
just to clean out your cookies,
let you know personally when
it's time to update your Antivirus.

They will let you know the trade secrets,
IMing you midday to mock the porn
some Marketing Guy downloaded
on his now broken laptop.

Later, in the break room,
when the same Marketing Guy
is seen intensely licking cream cheese
off the side of his bagel,

you and the I.T. guys will laugh
so hard, the receptionist will look up
and ask, *What? What? Did someone trip
and I missed it, y'all?*

FUCKING MADE EASY

Alarm, coffee,
shower, coffee,
clothes, coffee,
subway.

Subway, transfer, subway.
Coffee, office, elevator, computer.

Oh, oh, oh,
Daddy— no! Honey— no! Baby…
Yeah, I've never done this before.
Oh, yeah… yeah… yeah, yeah, yeah…
Delete. Delete. Delete.

Oh, baby, yeah. Take it out.
Let me see it. I want to see it.
I want to touch it. Coffee.
Let me taste it.

Come on! I'm hot.
I'm soo wet and I want you.
I want you to hurt me.

Oh, oh, oh! Oh, God! You're so big!
You're so hot! You're so big, and I am so wet.
I, delete, I, delete. Touch me. Just touch me.
Stick it in me! Stick it in my mouth!

I want to suck you off. Let me suck you off.

Let me… coffee. Let me… coffee. You're so big.

Let me taste it. I want it. I want you.
Ebay. Stick it in me. CNN.com. Stick in my ass!

Oh, God. Oh, God. Fuck me, fuck me, fuck me,
fuck me, fuck me, fuck me, fuck me, fuck me!
No, really: fuck *me*! Fuck my useless degree!
Fuck my disintegrating writing skills!
Fuck my ability to write anything but shitty porn!
Fuck.

Highlight. Delete. Delete. Delete. Coffee.

Coffee. Coffee. Come on… Come on…. Come on…
Cum on my face! That's right: cum on my face!
Then cum on my tits! Then cum on my ass!
Then cum in my ass! Oh yeah, I'm gonna cum,
I'm gonna cum, I'm gonna—

Word count too low.

Fuck.

Alright, alright. Coff—, alright. Coff— alright!

You like my friend? Let's bring her in.
Oh yeah! You like that? Great! Well, go ahead
and fuck her and I'll watch. I'll just sit here and watch!
And play with my big tits, my biiiiiig tits—

> Editorial note:
> Cristin, your erotica is getting increasingly—
> how should I put it—
> *antagonistic.*

> While an interesting take,
> the end product isn't coming across to us as—
> how should we put it—
> *erotica?*

All right. Fuck me.
Fuck me hard and fuck me quick.
Just whatever you do: Fuck me. Now.
Now! Now! Now! Now! Now!

Your cock is beautiful!
No, it's amazing! No, it's huge!
No, it's... all right, it's huge.

Ohhhhhhh! Mmmmmm!
It's so big! It's so hard!
You're so big! You're so hard!
It's so big! It's so hard!
Big! Hard! Big! Hard! Big!

Am I tight? Because you're huge.

All right, let's finish this, baby,
Because I want you... *still*
and it's getting late.

Coffee. I want you.
Coffee. I want you.
Coffee. I want you
to cum already.

Faster.
Let me suck it off a little.
Faster.
Let me suck you off.
Deadline.

I want you. I want you in me now.
I've never done this before.
Daddy, daddy.
It's so big.
Honey, baby.
I've never done this before.
I've never done this before.
Yeah, yeah, yeah, yeah!
Oh baby, oh baby, oh baby...
I'm gonna cum, I gonna cum, I'm gonna...

Point. Click. Save. Post.

Wait.

Then pay rent.

BALLAD OF THE LONELY

Holding hands is stupid.
Valentine's Day is stupid.
Dating while you are still in school is stupid.
Having sex in a car is stupid.
Having sex in a show is stupid.
Having sex in a fancy-schmancy hotel is stupid.
Giving or receiving flowers is stupid.
Giving or receiving oral sex is stupid,
unless you are receiving it,
and also you are a woman.
Boys who don't like me are stupid.
The boy who I like who doesn't like me is stupid.
Love is stupid.
Everything is stupid.
Except for this poem,
because the truth
can never be
stupid.

REAL LIVE PROMO II

Bush Country:</a>
Fetishism Guide Mona J. gets in the thick of it
with photos of women who prove hairy is beautiful.

How to Eat a Woman:</a>
Lesbian Erotica Guide Shelby G. shows how to make women
writhe under the power of your hot mouth.

Your Nude Boss is Tied to his Desk...</a>
You're horny, and a hot window washer appears.
What next? Read Straight Women's Erotica Guide's latest story.

BACK TO THE BASICS

It's a day job. It's a day job.
It's a day job. It's a day job.

It's fun to talk about at parties.
It can certainly make paying
the bills less of a challenge.

The poetry has been fun.

The ideas it puts in your head,
the dreams it can give you,
the strange hot hope it puts
in your winter, they are all
interesting perks for sure.

But I have to remember:
It's a job.

There is life after this.
There is a purpose to my writing
other than unique synonyms
for *tight*.

I need to remember that I can write
whole pages without using the words
tit or *cum* or *fucking*.

Although this poem
certainly hasn't helped
prove that point.

FALLING DOWN ON THE JOB

I have a bad heart.
I wish I were being poetic, but I'm not.
My heart sucks. Medically.

The last time I went in for a check-up,
my doctor couldn't find a pulse.

He tied my left arm up in a tourniquet,
pressed the stethoscope hard against it,
and said, *Now be quiet.*

Forty-five seconds passed.

Finally, the doctor lowered the stethoscope
and just stared at me. I exercise. I eat right.
I'm working in porn. Under the circumstances,
my heart should be pumping something strong.

But my heart is built like a bad excuse:
stumbling, weak, and makes you fall down
if you try to stand up too quickly.

I lost the bad excuse metaphor towards the end,
but you'll have to forgive me: I have a bad heart.

And no, I am not writing this poem because
I think having a bad heart is an interesting juxtaposition
for a poet to have, because I also have bad depth perception,
which arguably could be funnier and a lot less melodramatic
to write about.

No, I am writing this poem because I am on a plane
way way way above the earth and this canned air pressure
is making me feel really great, really really great and sparkly.
and since I don't drink or mess around with drugs,
I figure this will probably be the closest thing
I will ever have to writing a druggie poem.

What a disappointment.

CODA: *Turbulence! We are all going to die!*
Oh no, we're not... Well, then can I have more
coca-cola, Mr. Stewardess?
His answer: *No.*

LONG DISTANCE RELATIONSHIP

Hooray!
Look at me! I'm an *idiot!*
I'm in a long distance relationship!

Yeah! This rocks! I love being
really really really far away.
from him!

Really really really far away
from him all the time!

It's great!
Look at me! On the plane ride home!
I'm on the plane ride home and
I'm crying! This *rocks*!

I wish I could write more
but I'm crying too hard!
I mean,
I'm ROCKING too hard!

Life rules!

KEEPING IT IN NEUTRAL

Being able to work from home
when your long distance relationship
comes out for a visit seems pretty ideal.

Except when your job is porn,
and when you like to take your relationships
slow.

So I find it easier to just go to work.
Let him stay at home, watch the local kids shows
and drink the soda he can't get in Chicago.

Alone in my cubicle,
I will be the one to see all the weary nakedness,
the squeezing, arching, pushing in and pulling out,
will hear *ohhs* and *ahhs* and the *yes-yes-yes*'s.

In the evening, I will return to him, my heart
banging into his chest like a dog's happy tail.
Have you been thinking about me, he asks.

And I answer honestly.
Ooooh, I say, *Yes-yes-yes*.

LITTLE FACTORY

People say
it's porn.

How do
you know
if it's any
good?

I tell them
it's a pretty
simple thing
to figure out.

It either does it
for you, or
it doesn't.

It's porn,
so not all of it
will do it for you,
but most of it
will do it
for someone.

And me?
I'm like the foreman
at a little factory.

I don't put
the parts together,
but I make sure
things run
smoothly.

I keep
the workers
encouraged.

I say, *Imagine
the customers' faces
when they get a load
of this.*

UNDERSTANDING THE CUM SHOT

It's disgusting,
but necessary.

You really can't have
all the pumping,
all those positions,
all those grunts,
and moans and screams
without something
that brings it all together,
which loudly and definitively
says: *The End*.

Porn
without a cum shot
is like a sestina
without a BE/DC/FA
concluding stanza.

You just need to have
the familiar elements
repeated one last time
and with gusto!

Whoa.

This poem is proof
that I need to step away
from this laptop.

ON GETTING AN EMAIL FROM A HIGH SCHOOL GIRL TELLING ME SHE LOVES MY WRITING

This morning I woke up
and spent forty-five minutes
looking at an absolute rainbow
of cocks. Then I ate free Pop Tarts
and drank Yoohoo.

Later I checked my email,
and you were in my inbox,
shiny and generous.

I don't know you,
and yet I feel like
I'm disappointing you.

I want to hide from you
my marching band of porn poems,
loudly playing their horny tunes
in all my journals and soloing
in my performance sets.

Man, sometimes
I really have no idea
what the hell I am doing
with this life I call mine.

IT SHALL HENCEFORTH BE KNOWN #1

From this moment on,
it shall henceforth be known
that tampons shall no longer
be called "tampons."

They shall now be known
as "power rods."

As in:

"Man, my flow is so heavy,
I'm knocking out seven or eight
power rods a day!"

or

"Honey, while you're out,
can you pick me up a box
of power rods? A multi-pack
of power rods, please.
And remember:
only the power rods
with petal soft applicators.

I am a lady,
after all."

IT SHALL HENCEFORTH BE KNOWN #2

From this moment on,
it shall henceforth be known
that semen shall no longer
be called "semen."

It shall now be known
as "Gay Power Spray."

As in:

"Baby, I'm going to pull out
and spray Gay Power Spray
all over your boobs.
And then, I'm going to lick
my Gay Power Spray
off your boobs."

Because there is a new rule
that any time Gay Power Spray
is sprayed on a woman's body,
it must be licked off by the sprayer.

It is not cool to rub us down
with a towel or a tee-shirt,
like we're a middle-weight boxer
or some crap like that.

Oh no, you spray it,
you lick it.

Such is the way
of the Gay Power Spray.

IT SHALL HENCEFORTH BE KNOWN #3

From this moment on,
it shall henceforth be known
that female masturbation shall no longer
be called "female masturbation."

It shall now be known
as "rubbing one off."

As in:

"Baby, every time
a woman empowers herself
with sex-positive slang,
all I wanna do is rub one off
just for the fucking joy of it,
ya know?"

IT SHALL HENCEFORTH BE KNOWN #4

And lastly,

It shall henceforth be known
that "oral sex on a women"

otherwise known as "going down"
or "eating out,"

shall henceforth be referred to as

"the mandatory thing you have to do
in order to get any action whatsoever."

And that's pretty self-explanatory.

QUESTIONS BOYS ASK ME ABOUT MY JOB
(A PANTOUM)

I bet people ask you a lot dumb questions, right?
I bet people just freak out when you tell them what you do, right?
What does your boyfriend think?
Do you have a boyfriend?

I bet people just freak out when you tell them what you do, right?
Man, how do you even get a job like that?
Do you have a boyfriend?
Do you ever get to meet any of the stars?

Man, how do you even get a job like that?
Who's your favorite porn star?
Do you ever get to meet any of the stars?
Do you ever get turned on?

Who's your favorite porn star?
What do your parents think of this?
Do you ever get turned on?
Do you ever go to the bathroom during work and... ya know...

What do your parents think of this?
What does your boyfriend think?
Do you ever go to the bathroom during work and... ya know...
I bet people ask you a lot dumb questions, right?

THE MUSIC

So there's a lot of bass. So what?

If you want love-making to the sound
of flutes, then dial up some softcore,

you pussy.

NIETZSCHE

said that men should marry women
with whom they could see having
a conversation with for the rest
of their lives. Fuck sex, fuck beauty,
only words, thoughts and wit.
More people should read Nietzsche.

SASS MANIFESTO

My pussy is tired of being wet.

I'm not talking the physical state,
people, believe me.

No, I'm talking about the slang word: *wet*.

How come men get all the cool words
for sexual arousal like:
Hard and *Erect* and *Rarin' to 'Splode*.

And all we woman get is *wet*,
something which happens
to dogs and umbrellas.

And oh, what is this magical substance
causing us to get wet called?
Oh that's right, it's called our
wetness.

How original. We are made *wet*
by our *wetness*.

When I first started working as a writer
in porn, I thought I would encounter
different and far sexier terms for women
to use, but No! Everything's wet!

And the synonyms I found for *wetness*
were even worse, if you can imagine.
I am talking about *pussy juice,
pussy sauce, vaginal drippings,*
and I kid you not,

feminine mucus.

But then I realized: it's not porn's fault.

Because porn is like an 8-year-old boy,
and you'll have to follow me on this one,
it just calls things what it's heard
other people call them.

And that's when I knew it was up to me!
Up to me to change the world!
Or at least how the world refers to things
that come out of my pussy.

So I have done it here, people!
I have created a new female empowerment word
for *feminine wetness.*

And I'm doing my part.
I'm putting it in every porn story I write,
in every forum I monitor and
in every chatroom I'm forced to go into,

But it is not enough:
I need this to be a grassroots effort, people!

So, the next time you are making love to your lady,
or if you are a lady being made love to,
I need you to start using my new female empowerment word
for feminine wetness.

And that word is…

Sass.

That's right.

Sass.

It's a noun:
Lick my sass.

It's a verb:
I'm getting all sassed up.

And it's an adjective:
*Is it me, or does empowering yourself
through vocabulary get you all sassy?*

It's short! It's sweet!
It sounds great when grunted!

It's empowering for women to use,
and easy to remember for guys,
because, come on guys, it's only two letters!
And also it rhymes with ass.

And I know that some people think
it's silly to name something as frivolous
as sass, but I don't think women
are claiming their sexualities enough.

Men could fill up thesauruses with nicknames
for their balls, but we, women, don't even have
decent slang for our clits, perhaps
the most powerful organ in the entire universe!
The closet thing I've ever heard it called
is a *button*. Really? A button? It should be called
the *Mega-Power-Ultra-Rocket!* Or *The Vortex!*

It shouldn't be: *Baby, can you lick my button?*
It should be: *Time to spend an hour in The Vortex!*
I'll be tapping your head when I'm done!

But if we are going to start anywhere,
let's start where all good things start:
with a lot of *sass.*

Are you with me here, people? Are you ready
to bring this sassifric revolution to its feet?

Because I want every girl in America
to be proud of her pussy.

Every man in America to know the name
of what he's licking.

Every person in America to remember our motto:
If you want to make love with pride and class,
remember it's not wet anymore, *it's sass!*

SPULCHING

When I was 14,
the guy I liked wore a leather jacket
all the time, even in the summer,

and he knew things
my old middle school boyfriends
wouldn't even think of saying out loud.

Like Spulching:

Step one: find a dead girl.
Step two: drop heavy object on her abdomen
Step three: eat what comes out.

We never kissed,
and for good reason.

MORNING DATE

A night owl dating a morning person
works great if you live in different time zones.

After his night shift at his bookstore,
and his night shift at the neighborhood bars,
he calls me just as I am waking up.

We brush our teeth together,
watch the morning news.

Laughing, I put on my pants with one hand.
He tucks himself in two-thousand miles away.

I'm off to the porn mines, I say.
My dirty girl, he replies drowsily,
my dirty dirty girl.

COSTS

I can no longer watch old women
eat hot dogs, or watch women rub
their necks, tired on the subway home.

The happy groans after Thanksgiving
dinner seem overtly perverse.

When I get out of the shower
and look at myself in the mirror,
I can't help but wonder:
what's going to happen next?

THE CHRISTMAS PARTY

My aunt says,
So, you finally found a job,
after all that searching!

Yes, my mom replies for me,
and it's a dot com.

My aunt even knows the site,
she's been there before
for the horse riding section.

But tell her what you do there,
my mom says.

Ha-ha, Mom, I say.

She works in adult interest,
my mom says, *now you tell*
your aunt what that means.

It's moments like these
that I remember why I love
my dark-humored mom.
But it is Christmas, and even
Santa seems to be blushing.

I tell my aunt that adult interest
means I write about shuffleboard
and taxes.

She believes me, and it's enough
to make me believe
in Christmas miracles.

Outside, the snow falls
on that famous virgin and
her smiling newborn kid.

ORGASM HAIKUS
(ONLINE PORN VIDEO FOUND POETRY)

oooh ahhh ooohh ahhh oooh
yes yes that's right right there
oh oh oh oh aaaaah

don't stop fucking me
with that big black cock of yours
sweet lord jesus yes

you like this you like
this oh baby I'm ready
I'm ready ooooh fuck

yes yes yes yes yes
oh yes yes yes yes yes yes
oh oh yes fuck shit

take it take it oh
man oh shit man watch out I'm
gonna fucking pop

here it comes here it
comes I'm ready oooooh oh um
aahh here it comes: *squeak!*

oh oh oh hell no
come on hit it hit that thing
oh fuck man: *Mother!*

ASS SEX SESTINA
(A POP-UP AD FOUND POEM)

Do You like Anal?
Hot Teen Sluts Love Fucking!
Straight Up that Ass!
Who Doesn't Love DEEP Penetration?
Better than a PUSSY?
Soft Wet Ass Sliding Up and Down

Hot Ass Sex? Are You Down?
Click here for ANAL ANAL ANAL!!
What Cums After the PUSSY?
We Know You'll Love THIS Fucking!
Time for Chocolate Cherry Penetration!
First the Mouth, Then the Pussy, Then the ASS!

Hot Latina with Huge Perfect Ass!
Time for Back Door sex! Are You Down?
In her Ass, Out her Mouth: Anal Penetration!
Doggie-Style for Pussy and Anal!
Teens LOVE Anal Deep FUCKING!
Hardcore Anal Action! Don't be a Pussy!

Guy Bum Fucks a Hairy Pussy!
Deep Anal Penetration – Straight Up That Ass!
Watch the Whole Thing Go DOWN!
Whores LOVE that Anal Fucking!
Whores LOVE Fucking Anal!
Hot Brunette WHORE loves Anal Penetration!

Can You Hit the Bottom? Deep Anal Penetration!
Fresh Blonde Smooth Pussy!
Fresh Black Smooth Anal!
Teen Scared of Huge Dick in Ass!
Bitches Enjoy It! Suck It Down!
Amateurs Fucking! Fucking! Fucking!

Hot Teen Slut Love Sucking and Fucking!
Old Hot Whore Loves Deep Penetration!
HOT HOT HOT FUCKING! Scroll down!
Click Here for DRIPPING HOT PUSSY!
Three dicks? ONE ASS!
Interracial! BDSM! Oral! Anal!

Why Get Down? Why Not Start Fucking!
Do You Love Anal? Double Penetration?
Why Stick with Pussy, When You Can Have ASS!

CRISTINISABITTERBITCHASAURUS REX

My ex-boyfriend just discovered a new dinosaur.
He discovered a new type of dinosaur: a theropod.
This past summer, my ex-boyfriend went to China.
There he found a dinosaur bone, a foot bone,
just there, in the sand. Dug it up and brought it home,
to America, and that was it for months, nothing,
just a regular guy, just a regular old ex-boyfriend,
you know: life. And then, after months of normalcy,
it's discovered: *That ain't no ordinary dinosaur foot!*

It's a new dinosaur! A new theropod! Can you believe it?
What great news! A whole new dinosaur! A new theropod!
A whole new dinosaur foot! Thanks to my ex-boyfriend.

And what? The world said. *A new dinosaur?*
Quick, write him up in the Philadelphia Inquirer!
Quick, write him up in the Daily News!

What about me? chimed in Radio!
And me! said TV!

Hey, hey, hey! Don't rush him!
Don't rush our new dinosaur hero,
our new dinosaur discoverer! He found
a foot, a whole new dinosaur foot!

Query? Question? Yes? You?

Does he get to name the dinosaur?

Yes, he gets to name the dinosaur.
He gets to name it.

Cristin O'Keefe Aptowicz's ex-boyfriend
gets to name a motherfucking dinosaur.

Query? Question? Yes?

Who is Cristin O'Keefe Aptowicz?

Fifteen seconds of silence here as one
contemplates the question: If a girl's heart
breaks but her ex-boyfriend is too goddamn famous
to hear it, does she have the guts to off herself?

Who cares!

Cristin's Ex-Boyfriend is our new prince,
our new dinosaur prince!

This boy, this home-schooled beauty,
this red-cheeked dino-magican who produced
bone from sand, and a foot from that bone,
and from that foot, a whole new dinosaur!

We love him! A whole new dinosaur, you say!
Yes! A new theropod! A whole new dinosaur!
Well, ring out the ex-girlfriend bell!
Let dread fall like bricks! Karma not exist!
A whole new motherfucking dinosaur!
Praise praise praise!

And meanwhile,
somewhere in Astoria,
I am writing porn and
finishing my last can
of black bean soup.

PORN IS MY CO-PILOT

The day after I read about all the wonderful things
happening to the guy who broke my heart,

my boss told me I had to spend the day watching
the new videos uploaded on gay men's erotica.

I admit I felt a kinship with the poor bottoms,
being pounded on relentlessly

without even so much as a reach around.
I'm not sure what was more depressing:

being forced to watch gay sex videos on a day
when I'd rather stay in bed and cry,

or being so sad that I felt a kinship
with a gay sex video I'm watching.

And that's when it happened:
I heard his name. The ex-boyfriend's name.

I heard it through my headphones, and
it was being grunted. I felt immediately

better. It's true. Look, I believe in God, and
I believe that God can work in mysterious ways.

It may be sick but it's also true: I think God
sent me that video to remind me life is still cool.

And that life is still funny. That I'm still young.
And to tell other women this simple fact:

when you want to feel better about a guy
who fucked you over, then just watch a video

where a gay with the same name as your ex
is fucked by an enormous burly leather bear.

It's all right to smile, to hit the play button again
and again and again so you can grunt along:

Take it! Take it, you little bitch! Sometimes,
life can be better than you think.

REAL LIVE PROMO III.

Did You Vote?</a>
See why it's important that you did
as BDSM Guide James LiGate shows
how having fun in bed might put you in jail.

Forgot to Vote?</a>
Well, then someone here deserves a spanking!
Check out these hot links from Fetishism Guide Mona J.

THE BOX

It was a scam birthed
from a friendly convo
with some marketing guys
at the company holiday party.

They said, if I wanted,
they could get me samples
from the companies
which buy ads on my sites.

The day the box came,
the food editor received
a basket of expensive cheeses.

I would like to believe
it was the lindenberg
she was sniffing at,
when I passed around
the personal vibrators
in the conference room.

We all picked out
favorites and slapped
our money on the table.

The food editor squinted
through the plexiglass
as I won the whole pot
by correctly guessing that

the pink vibrating bear
would make it first
from one end of the
conference table to the other,
leaving its friends

the bullet, the bee,
the lipstick, the rabbit,
the egg, and the tiger

twitching in its wake.

LAID / OFF

People ask me a lot
if I think that working in the porn biz
has affected me negatively.

After all, I remain a virgin,
that kind of self-purity intact,
and I seem so well-adjusted
in my poetry, they say.

And the first thing I think of
is that I cannot watch
old women eating hot dogs.

I cannot watch old women
eating hot dogs and considering
I work in Times Square, it is
surprisingly hard to avoid.

Also, it seems as if I cannot watch
people stretching on the subway,
or the startled giggle of people accidently
bumping into each other on the street:
Oh, I'm sorry. Are you all right?

Other ordinary things that now
trigger job flashbacks include:

People enjoying their first bites
of something that tastes very good;

People awkwardly carrying
very furry dogs;

The sounds people make
when they first get into a cab
after they have been in the rain
for a very long time trying to hail one;

The nervous semi-pleased look
on a women's faces when they try on
an article of clothing for the first time
that they know looks good on them;

And people walking weiner dogs.

But today was the worst:
we had lay-offs at my job.

Even our company doesn't
seem immune to the bust
of the dot coms.

We lost one-third of our staff.
Cut. Suddenly, jobless.

There didn't seem to be
much logic to who was cut
although my crew and I,
we were held on.

Everyone was trying to keep it
together to say goodbye,
trying to comprehend
what was happening,

and all I could think, was
that this whole sad event
was like the world's most
depressing orgy.

All the faces, contorted, going,
Unngh, I can't believe it.

and the rubbing of necks,
and hugging each other exhaustedly,
and having optimism,
and apologizing a lot,
and sniffling that turned into laughter,
and laughter that turned into moans,

and exchanging of phone numbers
that will never be called,

and me, awkwardly in the corner,
never having experienced something
like this before,

me in the corner freezing up,
and not talking or touching anyone,
burying myself in work
after the most cursory
of goodbyes.

I'm afraid. I'm clearly afraid.
I don't want to be the bottom.
I want to stay on the top.

LIKE TUPPERWARE

was how the first friend of mine
who ever felt a guy's erect penis
described what it was like.

She punctuated her description
by rapping her knuckles on her pool table:
Oh God, like Tupperware!

Liar.

SIGNS OF THE DAUGHTER

Pop-ups
and their shy, sly brothers
the pop-unders,
come with the territory.

Cookies (the term
for the information stored
without your permission
on your computer which tracks
what sites you go to and in turn
influences the banner ads
you get) are also
par for the course.

However, when your mother
comes to visit for the weekend,
you have to tell your boss
you can't work during the weekend
and beg the I.T. guys to give
your computer a thorough cleaning.

The I.T. guys do you one better
by actually installing cookies
so the banners and pop-ups
are for clever books and news sites.
You guess they've been down
this road before.

Still, all weekend long,
you nervously watch as your mom
checks CNN.com and googles
the best restaurants in Queens.
The computer stays clean:
a miracle.

Still, when your mother remembers
reading an article in the *New York Times*
about a place in Queens that sells
the biggest, hottest sausage in NYC,
you have to ask her to step away
from the Google search box,
realizing she wouldn't be prepared
to swallow what your computer
would have given her.

I COULD MAKE MONEY OFF THOSE TITS

I was crossing Astoria Boulevard when he said it.

I am not sure which one of the 40-year-old chain-smoking gas station attendants actually spit out the phrase. They were all yelling at me, clicking their tongues against their teeth as I dashed by. But one them of, perhaps realizing that I wasn't going to turn around no matter what they said, one of them just out and said it:

I could make money off those tits.

The intonation was so muddy, I couldn't tell if he wanted to make money off my tits, or just wanted my tits to make money off them, or just to have my tits in general. And though I nearly wanted to stop and clarify, I didn't. I just kept walking, because I don't need to be thinking of making money off these tits anymore. I have a job.

Within weeks of starting my smutty position, my mom began sending me decorations for my cubicle. Still stuck in the same IRS building that has been her second home since I was seven, she wanted to decorate my office space in NYC, seven floors up from Times Square. And so her Philadelphia Water Department magnets and velcro-fisted Christmas monkeys (bought from the seasonal aisle of our neighborhood CVS) fight for attention, while I sit in my ergonomically correct chair, laptop on lap, earphones in ears, and from the belly of my computer comes… cums:

> *Oh yeah, oh yeah, yeah, yeah…*
> *right there…*

and

> *Mandy. Mandy, Mandy, Mandy,*
> *you're a naughty little girl.*

and

Cum on my face! Cum on my face!
Now cum on my face!

And I have to take it seriously, watching over my twelve erotica
guides like they were my own fussy children: helping them get
their money if the finance department is being a bunch of bullies;
copyediting their spelling and grammar; and calming them down
when they get frustrated.

REAL EXCHANGE:

Him:
I can't! I can't! I can't!
I can't think of any more ideas.
I'm stuck. I'm through.

Me:
Now hold on there, Austin,
one of the top subjects on your site right now
is interracial blowjobs. How about we brainstorm
about that for a while? Okay? Like,
how about a "We Are The World"
blowjob-only orgy? Or what about
"Gloryholes Across America"?
You are just frustrated because
you have done all you can with anal sex,
but honey, that's not the end of the road!

Did I mention I am getting paid for this?

However, there is always that terrible moment when I have to tell
a feminist friend about what I do for a living. I know the response
rocketing across her face must have mirrored my own, that first time
my best friend told me that she had decided to work at Hooters.

My best friend: the hardworking college student, the devoted girlfriend, the stone cold fox who used to grab the cell phones of men who catcalled her and scream into the phone, *Do you know what he just said to me?* until finally all the business men in her neighborhood zipped up their car windows and silently watched her walk down the street, her body like a machine that accidentally sprayed eroticism all over the place.

It was impossible to think that *this* woman, that this best friend of mine would don a white and orange owl-crested tank-top and a pair of teeny tiny orange basketball? shorts to serve beers, wings, and nachos to men who would order more and more and more so that she would serve it to them, bending at the waist to give them a better look at her creamy, full cleavage, bending at the waist as specifically spelled out in the Hooters Handbook, along with rules, like:

1. You are never allowed to tuck your hair behind your ears.

2. You are never allowed in the kitchen.

3. You must never wear underwear under your shorts.

When she told me, I am sure there was that same contortion of my eyes and nose and mouth; my face was a machine that sprayed confusion and contempt all over the Hooters outfit she showed me, and all I could think was: *Why?*

Why are you setting us back 25 years? Why do you want to become a body that some manager —actually named Tito!— will feel free to control? Tito, who told you to do 200 crunches a night to get rid of "that belly" and to get a tan, while you're at it. A man who looked at you, and thought, *I could make money off those tits...*

And when I finally did ask, *Why?*

She said, *Tips.*

And then she said, *And it's fun.*

And I could only imagine what my face looked like when she said, *Fun.*

Could only imagine until I got this job: Guide Manager for Adult Interest.

My friends who have called me at work say that in my voice mail message, I emphasize the Adult Interest in my title, making it stand out, elongating it: *Ah-dult In-ter-rrrrr-est.*

My presence in the office has seemed to validate Adult Interest: making it more fun, less dirty, like the spread in the Lesbian Erotica section of Jade, who looks like she accidentally got naked, and accidentally spilled milk all over her body, laughing with her hands on her hips, smiling, nose-wrinkled, covered in milk, looking at me, and I think: *I could make money off those tits.*

And I am. A lot. Copy-editing, slinging videos up, writing pun-filled promo and I am having fun. A lot. Watching people get naked, get together, get happy. Listening to the audio on earphones like a dirty secret, which it is, but isn't. Being introduced to the new girl in the office while fisting videos are being downloaded onto my hard-drive.

This is my life, nine-to-five, Monday through Friday: free coffee, free donuts, free porn.

And the obvious question is: *How does this make you feel?*

Women as object, women as fuck machine, women as slut, women as stereotype, women as hole, women as girl, women as moneymaker, spread-open cum-gobbler.

You promote this, promote them. You make money off of women just like you, or your sister, or your mother. You make money off of women who deserve to be valued more than just a hot, wet receptacle for cock.

And I say, *Look, all porn isn't about devaluing women, just like all poetry isn't just about egotistical masturbating.*

And I say to them, *The number three site on our service is "Straight Women's Erotica." And the number two site is "Gay Men's Erotica." And the number one site is "Amateur Erotica."*

These sites are not dedicated to the men who shout at me at gas stations. Not dedicated to seeing how many cocks can be stuck in my mouth or how much semen I can rub on my breasts.

They are dedicated to liberation:

Hey, women: you can have fun with sex too!

Hey, guys: you can love another man, and it is okay!

And you, anonymous you: you can be beautiful too, without implants, or airbrushing, or a stupid porn smile!

In Amateur Erotica, men and women post photos on our sites of themselves, naked, and ask: *Am I beautiful? Would you love me?* And overwhelmingly, every single person responds: *Yes! Yes, you are so beautiful! You are the most beautiful person I've seen today!* And they mean it.

And yes, sometimes I come across things that are ugly and cruel, things that validate every terrible thing that porn has to offer. But I feel like I have an opportunity to help the beautiful and the empowering to kick down some doors.

I feel like I can liberate porn from its five-hundred-cocks-in-one-night, bad-boy status, and show the world that porn can be fun, that it should be fun, that it *is* fun. That some days we should all get naked, accidentally cover ourselves in milk, wrinkle our noses and smile, simply because we are the most beautiful people we know.

Now, every person of consenting age I see walking down the street these days, I think to myself: *I could make money off those tits.* Every man, every woman, no matter the size, or the age, or how beautiful they think they are. Now, they are all so beautiful to me. Every person, I think, I could make money off those tits. Yes, I could make money.

REAL LIVE PROMO IV

A Lesson Gore Should Have Learned:</a>
Lesbian Erotica Guide Shelby G. gives you six different ways to lick bush.

Forget Bush:</a>
Escape from politics for a while
with Gay Men's Erotica Guide Austin Aleksander's week of hard hung men.

LET'S MAKE OUT!
(OR THE LOVE POEM I WAS SURPRISED I COULD STILL WRITE AFTER SO MANY MONTHS OF WORKING IN PORN)

Hey you, with the Wonka Tee-shirt,
the weiner dog and the sneakers
that say "What Me Worry?!"

Let's make out!

It's y2k1, baby,
time for the heavy petting revolution to begin
and I want it to begin with us.

Unngggh!

Let's get freaky
over-the-clothes-style.

I want to *Romper Room* together
until your parents start knocking
on the basement door.

Let me suck on your neck
until the blood in your vein explodes,
and then gets trapped into the third layer
of your epidermis and then you can't do anything
about it because you're a straight boy and
you don't have any make-up, and
everyone you see just looks at you
and goes:

> *Damn, what the hell happed to you?*
> *Were you attacked by an animal?*

And you can answer:

Yes.

Unngggh!

I want us to be the spokespeople for making out.

Make public "making out appearances"
in the Plastic Colored Ball Pen
at the local McDonalds,

get caught necking
in the Self Help section
of the Barnes and Noble,

and grind against
the walls of the 23rd St. station
until the N starts running local again.

Unngggh!

I want to make out at an orgy.
I want to make out at a funeral.
I want to make out at a poetry slam.

I want us to represent making out
the way light bulbs represent ideas;
the way Picasso represents cubism;
and the way horniness represents me!

Unngggh!

I want us to bring back dry humping
like Tarantino brought back Travolta.

Because you get me worked up
in a not-getting-past-second-base way.

Unngggh!

You get me worked up in that,
I-want-to-get-gentle-all-over-your-forehead way.

Unngggh!

And when we lay down
on your vintage Star Wars bedsheets,
you get me worked up in that
running-my-fingers-up-and-down
the-sides-of-your-body-until
we-both-get-frustrated-and-stop
way.

Unngggggggggggggggggggggggggh!

Let's make out, baby,

Because sex is a four letter word,
minus one letter.

But make out is a four letter word,
plus three.

GETTING OFF EARLY

The truth? I was laid off
shortly after my company got rid
of the porn sites entirely.

Our flailing dot com
was bought out by a media empire
who also owned a kids TV channel
which was only shown in schools.

Their company spreadsheets
couldn't handle all that my sites
had to bring. Or at least,
that's what their PR people said.

A month before I was to be laid off
(although I didn't know that then)
my boss heard that I had written poems
about my time working for porn.

He begged me to perform them.
When I wouldn't, he collected
money from co-workers who also
wanted to see me perform the poems
and pretty soon, there was kitty
worth as much as a day's pay.

The truth? I couldn't say no,
and performed on the top of my desk.
It felt ridiculous. It felt like old-school dot com.
It felt astonishingly good.

The day I was laid off,
I wasn't even in the office.
I got the phone call from home
as I was leaving for Australia,

a trip that was being paid
for by a Melbourne Arts Center
so that I could perform poetry
for their community.

This being the situation,
I honestly couldn't feel that bad
about being laid off.

But the truth? I'm working class.
so losing a job hurts no matter what.

Still, I knew that I lost the job
a long time ago, when I had to
approve the letter letting our editors
know our beautiful and vulgar little sites
were being shut down; when I wrote
the copy letting visitors know
the sad news too; when I said goodbye
to my lusty days and nights,
the silly raw humanity of it;

And said hello to copyediting movie reviews.
Life. A real job.

That morning I was laid off,
I remember the shiny shock of it,
the nervous grin appearing on my face.

The transparent understanding
of my voice on the phone:
Sure sure sure.
Hey, you gotta do what you gotta do.
Uh-huh.

Later that day,
I got on a huge silver plane
to fly me halfway around the world
to perform my own words
to a sea of strange amazing faces.

I remember looking
out the window and thinking:
Remember this moment.
This is a good moment.
Remember this moment
forever.

I closed my eyes
as the plane lifted off.

Behind me was New York City,
forms to be filled out for unemployment,
and a laptop hopelessly choked with porn.

Ahead of me was a bright sky,
an upside-down world, and the truth:
that I had a new life smiling down at me,
an endless spiral of clean poems
just waiting to be written.

ACKNOWLEDGMENTS

Grateful acknowledgements also are made to the following anthologies and journals, in which some of these writings first appeared in slightly different forms:

The Last American Valentine – "Long Distance Relationship"
Long Shot – "Sass Manifesto"
The Legendary – "Ass Sex Sestina," "Sass Manifesto" and "Orgasm Haikus"

Grateful acknowledgements are also made to the following CDs and podcasts in which audio of the following poems have also appeared:

IndieFeed Performance Poetry Podcast (performancepoetry.indiefeed. com) – "Fucking Made Easy"
Urbana: Bowery Poetry Club (CD) – "Sass Manifesto"
Urbana: New High Score (CD) – "Long Distance Relationship"

Lastly, grateful acknowledgements are made to **Steve Marsh** and **The Wordsmith Press**, who published an earlier edition of this book.

ABOUT THE AUTHOR

CRISTIN O'KEEFE APTOWICZ is the author of four other books of poetry: *Dear Future Boyfriend, Working Class Represent, Oh, Terrible Youth* and *Everything is Everything*. She is also the author of the non-fiction book, *Words In Your Face: A Guided Tour Through Twenty Years of the New York City Poetry Slam*, which *The Washington Post* named as one of five Notable Books on Exploring Poetry in 2008. Born and raised in Philadelphia, Aptowicz moved to New York City at the age of 17. At age 19, she founded the three-time National Poetry Slam championship poetry series NYC-Urbana, which is still held weekly at the NYC's famed Bowery Poetry Club. Most recently, Aptowicz was named the 2010-2011 ArtsEdge Writer-In-Residence at the University of Pennsylvania.

For more information, please visit her website:
www.aptowicz.com

NEW WRITE BLOODY BOOKS FOR 2011

DEAR FUTURE BOYFRIEND
A Write Bloody reissue of Cristin O'Keefe Aptowicz's first book of poetry

HOT TEEN SLUT
A Write Bloody reissue of Cristin O'Keefe Aptowicz's second book of poetry
about her time writing for porn

WORKING CLASS REPRESENT
A Write Bloody reissue of Cristin O'Keefe Aptowicz's third book of poetry

OH, TERRIBLE YOUTH
A Write Bloody reissue of Cristin O'Keefe Aptowicz's fourth book of poetry
about her terrible youth

38 BAR BLUES
A collection of poems by C.R .Avery

WORKIN' MIME TO FIVE
Humor by Derrick Brown

REASONS TO LEAVE THE SLAUGHTER
New poems by Ben Clark

YESTERDAY WON'T GOODBYE
New poems by Brian Ellis

WRITE ABOUT AN EMPTY BIRDCAGE
New poems by Elaina M. Ellis

THESE ARE THE BREAKS
New prose by Idris Goodwin

BRING DOWN THE CHANDELIERS
New poems by Tara Hardy

THE FEATHER ROOM
New poems by Anis Mojgani

LOVE IN A TIME OF ROBOT APOCALYPSE
New poems by David Perez

THE NEW CLEAN
New poems by Jon Sands

THE UNDISPUTED GREATEST WRITER OF ALL TIME
New poems by Beau Sia

SUNSET AT THE TEMPLE OF OLIVES
New poems by Paul Suntup

GENTLEMAN PRACTICE
New poems by Buddy Wakefield

HOW TO SEDUCE A WHITE BOY IN TEN EASY STEPS
New poems by Laura Yes Yes

OTHER WRITE BLOODY BOOKS (2003 - 2010)

STEVE ABEE, GREAT BALLS OF FLOWERS (2009)
New poems by Steve Abee

EVERYTHING IS EVERYTHING (2010)
New poems by Cristin O'Keefe Aptowicz

CATACOMB CONFETTI (2010)
New poems by Josh Boyd

BORN IN THE YEAR OF THE BUTTERFLY KNIFE (2004)
Poetry collection, 1994-2004 by Derrick Brown

I LOVE YOU IS BACK (2006)
Poetry compilation (2004-2006) by Derrick Brown

SCANDALABRA (2009)
New poetry compilation by Derrick Brown

DON'T SMELL THE FLOSS (2009)
New Short Fiction Pieces By Matty Byloos

THE BONES BELOW (2010)
New poems by Sierra DeMulder

THE CONSTANT VELOCITY OF TRAINS (2008)
New poems by Lea C. Deschenes

HEAVY LEAD BIRDSONG (2008)
New poems by Ryler Dustin

UNCONTROLLED EXPERIMENTS IN FREEDOM (2008)
New poems by Brian Ellis

CEREMONY FOR THE CHOKING GHOST (2010)
New poems by Karen Finneyfrock

POLE DANCING TO GOSPEL HYMNS (2008)
Poems by Andrea Gibson

CITY OF INSOMNIA (2008)
New poems by Victor D. Infante

THE LAST TIME AS WE ARE (2009)
New poems by Taylor Mali

IN SEARCH OF MIDNIGHT: THE MIKE MCGEE HANDBOOK OF AWESOME (2009)
New poems by Mike McGee

OVER THE ANVIL WE STRETCH (2008)
New poems by Anis Mojgani

ANIMAL BALLISTICS (2009)
New poems by Sarah Morgan

NO MORE POEMS ABOUT THE MOON (2008)
NON-Moon poems by Michael Roberts

MILES OF HALLELUJAH (2010)
New poems by Rob "Ratpack Slim" Sturma

SPIKING THE SUCKER PUNCH (2009)
New poems by Robbie Q. Telfer

RACING HUMMINGBIRDS (2010)
New poems by Jeanann Verlee

LIVE FOR A LIVING (2007)
New poems by Buddy Wakefield

WRITE BLOODY ANTHOLOGIES

THE ELEPHANT ENGINE HIGH DIVE REVIVAL (2009)
Poetry by Buddy Wakefield, Derrick Brown,
Anis Mojgani, Shira Erlichman and many more!

THE GOOD THINGS ABOUT AMERICA (2009)
An illustrated, un-cynical look at our American Landscape. Various authors.
Edited by Kevin Staniec and Derrick Brown

JUNKYARD GHOST REVIVAL (2008)
Poetry by Andrea Gibson, Buddy Wakefield, Anis Mojgani,
Derrick Brown, Robbie Q, Sonya Renee and Cristin O'Keefe Aptowicz

THE LAST AMERICAN VALENTINE:
ILLUSTRATED POEMS TO SEDUCE AND DESTROY (2008)
24 authors, 12 illustrators team up for a collection of non-sappy love poetry.
Edited by Derrick Brown

LEARN THEN BURN (2010)
Anthology of poems for the classroom. Edited by Tim Stafford and Derrick Brown.

LEARN THEN BURN TEACHER'S MANUAL (2010)
Companion volume to the *Learn Then Burn* anthology. Includes lesson plans and worksheets for educators.
Edited by Tim Stafford and Molly Meacham.

WWW.WRITEBLOODY.COM

WRITEBLOODY

QUALITY AMERICAN BOOKS

PULL YOUR BOOKS UP BY THEIR BOOTSTRAPS

Write Bloody Publishing distributes and promotes great books of fiction, poetry and art every year. We are an independent press dedicated to quality literature and book design, with an office in Long Beach, CA.

Our employees are authors and artists so we call ourselves a family. Our design team comes from all over America: modern painters, photographers and rock album designers create book covers we're proud to be judged by.

We publish and promote 8-12 tour-savvy authors per year. We are grass-roots, D.I.Y., bootstrap believers. Pull up a good book and join the family. Support independent authors, artists and presses.

Visit us online:
WRITEBLOODY.COM

CPSIA information can be obtained
at www.ICGtesting.com
Printed in the USA
FSOW01n2327121214
3817FS